FACING
SON
THE

FACING SON THE

KRIS BELCHER

DESERET
BOOK

Salt Lake City, Utah

DESERET BOOK is a registered trademark of Deseret Book Company.

Visit us at DeseretBook.com

Library of Congress Cataloging-in-Publication Data

Belcher, Kristin Warner, author.
  Facing the Son : eliminating the spiritual light blockers in your life / Kristin Warner Belcher.
      pages   cm
  Includes bibliographical references and index.
  ISBN 978-1-60908-066-2 (paperbound)
  1. Christian life—Mormon authors.   I. Title.
  BX8656.B45 2011
  248.4'893—dc23   2011016866

Printed in the United States of America
R. R. Donnelley, Crawfordsville, IN

10   9   8   7   6   5   4   3   2   1

To my sweet husband, James,
who has the best vision of any
man I've ever met.

CONTENTS

CONTENTS

INTRODUCTION

The light of dawn signaled the morning of the Sabbath, but the glow of the sun meant nothing to him. From his seat at the side of the dusty road, the beggar felt the sun's heat warming his back and just a hint of breeze touching his upturned face. For many years, he had sat in darkness, each day coming to this same spot of ground. Here he begged from the many passersby for his subsistence. His eyes saw nothing, but his ears followed the sounds of movement near him—sounds of animals and their masters, mothers calling after their children, and the shuffling of feet as people walked by.

He listened as a group of men approached. They stopped and spoke together about his blindness. He marveled at the words of one whom the others called Jesus, when they asked, "Master, who did sin, this man, or his parents, that he was born blind?"

In anticipation, the blind man leaned forward to catch the reply.

"Jesus answered, Neither hath this man sinned, nor his parents: but that the works of God should be made manifest in him" (John 9:2–3).

He couldn't believe it. Never before had the blind man heard someone teach such a thing, but the words rang true in his heart. He had not deserved this physical problem; he knew it. He had always known it. Yet now this man preached what he had felt from his childhood.

This Jesus, who called himself "the light of the world" (John 9:5), spoke kindly to the beggar as He stooped before him. The beggar heard the stranger spit in the dirt, and then he felt warm, wet clay cover his blind eyes. He drew back, not understanding but somehow not fearing this new stranger. He heard a crowd begin to gather as Jesus helped him to his feet and quietly gave him instructions to "go, wash in the pool of Siloam" (John 9:7).

The beggar, now urged forward by some new feeling inside, was assisted to the pool. A glimmer of hope pricked his heart, but still, he was uncertain what would happen as he entered the water.

The blind man did as he was commanded and washed off the clay. Instantly, the light of the sun met his eyes and filled his mind. Never before had he ever imagined such brightness. Familiar objects and people appeared foreign with their vivid colors and strange dimensions, yet these new sights brought him unbelievable joy. Tears of amazement and gratitude spilled down his cheeks. It was a miracle. His eyes had been opened.

I have always loved reading the New Testament story of how Christ healed the blind man. I have imagined what that day would have been like, what the man may have been feeling, and the compassion that must have shown on the face of Jesus. Having struggled with very limited eyesight throughout my life and finally gone completely blind in 2003, I have longed to receive such a healing.

As a college student at Brigham Young University, when I still possessed some vision in one eye, I was present in a religion class where we were told that the prophet, President Ezra Taft Benson, was in the building next door. After class, if we waited outside, in an hour, we might catch a glimpse of him. When class ended, I was amazed to see that no one besides me had remained to see the prophet.

I sat in the sun—just waiting. It occurred to me that if

I was the only one around when President Benson exited the building, perhaps I could not only see him but speak with him as well. I had read and heard of many modern-day miracles that had been done by the hands of apostles and prophets in our day. Was it possible that I could receive a miracle and, through the power of the priesthood held by this prophet, be healed? Would President Benson take time to give me a blessing? Would Father in Heaven cause my sight to be improved or even fully restored?

Now, perhaps this sounds a bit Pollyannaish, or even foolish, but I knew that God worked through His prophets and that such a healing, according to the will of the Lord and my faith, was absolutely possible.

Finally, when the doors to the building were opened, students seemed to come out of nowhere, clustering to see the prophet. I was pushed to the rear of the crowd, and I watched President Benson shake the hands of those in the front row. My heart was saddened as I saw my chance to speak with the prophet, and possibly be healed by him, pass me by.

However, as I joined the group in celebrating President Benson's birthday by singing to him, the Spirit comforted me and taught me an unforgettable lesson.

It was not the will of the Father that I should be healed of my sight impairment. Understanding entered my mind, as it so often had before, through the words of a scripture. I thought and felt the power of Christ's teaching to His disciples on that day when He healed the blind man so long ago, "Neither hath this man sinned, nor his parents: but that the works of God should be made manifest in him" (John 9:3).

Instead of receiving complete healing, it was my mission to keep my sight impairment. I learned through the Spirit that as I struggled with my disability, others would see the help given me by the hand of the Lord, and this would help them seek Christ in their own lives. This was not the answer I had hoped for and wanted, but I gathered my courage and received strength to move forward.

Since that time, the passage in John 9 has given me purpose amidst my struggles. Yet that is not all. As I have studied this chapter in more depth, I have come to realize that the healing of the beggar was not the primary focus of the passage. The man who was blind served as a living lesson for a deeper truth—the need to overcome spiritual blindness in order to truly see what is important.

After the beggar was healed, he was taken before the Pharisees and questioned. Because Christ had healed this man on the Sabbath, the Pharisees charged Him with breaking the law of Moses and condemned him of being of the devil. They totally missed the miracle and the power of the miracle worker. The Pharisees were blind to all but their own interpretation of the law. They could see with their physical eyes, yet they were blind—blind to what mattered most: Jesus Christ.

It seems so easy for me to diagnose the vision problem of the Pharisees. Why couldn't they, why didn't they recognize or focus on the Savior? Why did they see only the law and not the giver of it? Yet, I wonder how many times I do the same thing. How often do I allow other things, even personal feelings, to take my focus away from spiritual matters and ultimately from my Savior? Spiritually speaking, what is my visual acuity? Do I suffer from a spiritual blindness similar to that of the Pharisees?

How can you and I improve our spiritual vision so that we can grow closer to the Savior?

I believe the sun can shed some light on this for us. After I lost my eyesight, I went through light withdrawals. I missed the sunlight in the clear blue sky, the sunrise over the mountains, and the beautiful colors of a sunset. Now, when I go outside, the only way I know if the sun is shining is if I feel it on my skin. I love to feel the warmth of the sun's rays on my face. There is a comfort in that feeling.

The sun can also provide valuable direction. I learned this in the Orientation and Mobility class that I attended after I first went blind. The goal of the course was for me to navigate safely and independently using a white cane.

In one lesson, I was taught that I can determine what direction I am facing by using the sun. Here's how it works. If it were morning, and I felt the sun's warmth on my right-hand side, then I would know I was facing north. Similarly, if I felt the warmth on my back, I would know I was facing west. This information can be vitally important to my navigation and safety.

Spiritually, we can also receive comfort and direction from the Son. If we can feel the warmth of the Son—the Spirit—then we know we are facing the right direction. However, if we aren't feeling that warmth, we can be certain that we need a course correction. This information is vital to our eternal progression.

As we face the Son and seek His light, you and I can gain access to real power. We can have a greater ability to "see" solutions to difficult problems, receive hope when life appears hopeless, obtain the enabling power of grace to accomplish seemingly impossible tasks, receive forgiveness from sin, and gain strength to endure trials faithfully. We can do this incrementally each day as we seek and apply true principles to aid us in real, day-to-day experiences.

Let's look at how an increased ability to see spiritually can affect us in a typical day's experience. Each day, I interact with my children, and often my patience is tried. When I grow irritated at their whining, complaining, or arguing, and I let that irritation fester, then I am not facing the Son. I am allowing the light of the Spirit to be eclipsed. However, if I have an automatic plan to engage when I begin feeling such irritation, then I can more easily think, feel, and act with love from the unobstructed light source: Jesus Christ. This will help me handle the situation with more patience, in a Christlike manner and without contention—at least on my end. I will see more clearly because the darkness that comes from holding onto negative feelings is replaced by spiritual light and strength.

I invite you to try examining your own visual acuity—not your physical sight, for that is of lesser importance, but your spiritual ability to see. How is this done? I have found that spiritual vision may be easier to identify if I compare it to the different stages of physical vision I have gone through in my life.

At the age of seven months, I was diagnosed with bilateral retinoblastoma—multiple tumors on the retinas of both eyes. This cancer was treated with radiation therapy, and my life and some vision were saved.

For the first eight or nine years of my life, I had limited vision in both eyes, but my retinas were very scarred, leaving me with blind spots in my field of vision. However, until I ran into something, I didn't notice the blind spots. My mind adapted so that I just looked around them automatically.

When I lost the sight in my left eye, due to a cataract and calcification of my pupil, I depended solely on the vision that remained in my right eye. It was difficult to rely on less light than I had been used to, and I didn't like the feeling of darkness. Then, when my left optic nerve died, it grew even darker, if possible, and it was like part of me was lost to a blank void. My world grew smaller and smaller.

With these changes came the need to make adjustments to help me utilize my remaining vision. For example, I turned my head to the left so that I could see what was in front of me and not just what was on my right-hand side.

I developed a cataract on the lens of my right eye when I was in high school, and surgery was required to improve my sight. My lens was removed and an artificial lens was put in its place. Consequently, everything appeared brighter. The cloudy lens had dimmed my vision, but I hadn't noticed because the change had occurred so gradually. With the new lens, colors seemed brighter and more vibrant. I literally felt as though I had more light in my life.

Then, when I was thirty-two years old, the remaining vision in my right eye began to fade, and I was diagnosed with more cancer. This time, the tumors were behind my right eye and had been caused by the radiation I had received as an infant. Despite many surgeries and even more faith and prayers, I lost my sight when it became necessary to remove my right eye in order to remove the cancer. I then was completely blind—left in absolute darkness. I was devastated.

At different times throughout our mortal lives, we may, depending on our faithfulness, experience differing degrees of spiritual vision. Clear vision requires that there be no obstruction to light. However, we are constantly bombarded by temptation and sin, which, if chosen or embraced, will obstruct our view.

I wonder if you and I get so used to these light-blockers that we begin to look around them, until that becomes so automatic that we don't even notice them. Or perhaps we make small bad choices that don't appear to change our vision but that, if not corrected, dim our sight. If we stray further and further from the Light—Jesus Christ—we can feel spiritually as I did physically when I lost all vision: left in darkness and despair. The light we previously enjoyed may seem lost forever.

If we honestly identify and properly treat those things that blind us spiritually, our focus on Christ will sharpen, and our vision will become clearer. Through the help of the Spirit and the power of the Atonement, we can improve our ability to see spiritually in this life and to make it through the difficulties and darkness of mortality.

As you and I seek light together, I know that the Spirit will lead us to actions appropriate to our own situations and spiritual acuity. I know that as we work to improve our spiritual sight, praying for the help and direction of heaven, darkness will retreat and we will move closer to the Light. For Christ is the only cure, remedy, and healer of our spiritual vision. He has promised, "I will bring the blind by a way that they knew not; I will lead them in paths that they have not known: I will make darkness light before them, and crooked things straight. These things will I do unto them, and not forsake them" (Isaiah 42:16).

Chapter 1

FACE THE SON BY REMEMBERING YOUR IMPORTANCE

Light-Blockers: Everyday Emotions, Attitudes, and Behaviors

I t was to be my greatest role ever! True, I was only in the sixth grade, but my part as Jumbo the Elephant in the school play would launch my acting career for sure. I was to share the large gray elephant costume with my friend Katie, who would be the two front legs and head, while I was the back legs and rear end. Hmm. I hope that wasn't typecasting.

We were to sing a beautiful duet as Jumbo with an English accent, and we felt like stars as we practiced. But a few days before the performance, Katie got the chicken pox, and I was left to play the part of the pachyderm alone. Although I felt sorry for my friend, I was secretly thrilled for my chance to shine. I was promoted from the rear end of Jumbo to be the entire animal. I would now wear the papier-mâché elephant head as well as the tail, and it would be exclusively my English-accented song that would sound from the cardboard-paper-towel-tube trunk. I was nervous but very excited.

The big night arrived, and I sang proudly in the chorus. Midway through the play, a few minutes before I would make my debut as Jumbo, disaster struck. A student on the front row of the risers stole my thunder. Right in the middle of our performance, he threw up. Yuck! Then, as he made his way toward the wings, midstride, he once again vomited on the stage. Talk about a showstopper! The entire audience was stunned into complete silence.

For several moments, no one moved. At last, a member of the audience came onstage to clean up the mess. When his job was complete, he whispered to all of us on the risers, "The show must go on!"

That was it! All my dreams of stardom—vanished with the vomit!

The show did go on, and I sang my well-rehearsed part; however, I was not the star, as I had anticipated. When my would-be legendary night is recalled, it is the boy on the risers with the flu and the volunteer janitor (my father) who claim the spotlight.

I was very disappointed at my failed attempt at stardom.

I guess Jumbo wasn't to be my greatest role after all. There have been many times since my Jumbo days that I have wondered about the roles I fill: like when I crawl into bed after a long, difficult day with my children, certain that the Mother of the Year award definitely won't be bestowed on me. Or when I have taught a class at church and am pretty sure it totally flopped. Ever felt this way?

These and other roles, however, are secondary, supporting roles to the most important role we will ever fill in this life. It is who we are. We are divine children of the Eternal Father. This role is glorious, and we never need feel disappointment in it. We are growing and progressing in order to become like Him, and this includes working on our ability to see spiritually.

Since I lost my eyesight, I have been asked many times, "What is the hardest part about being blind?" My answer? "Not seeing." It's true—sarcastic, but true. It is difficult to live in total darkness. I have no access to light whatsoever, and I'm powerless to change my situation.

Similarly, the hardest part and most spiritually damaging consequence of spiritual blindness is our decreased ability to access the light of the Son. We are directed and comforted by the Savior through the influence and power of the Holy Ghost, and unless we think and act in worthy ways, we can exclude ourselves from that influence. This can leave us without the help and comfort we may need today, as well as the direction we so desperately need to return to our Father in Heaven. However, in this situation, unlike my physical blindness, we do have power to change. We can face the Son and seek His light—the light available to us because of our role as God's children.

Unlike some kinds of physical blindness, we are born with clear spiritual vision. As children of Heavenly Father, it is our challenge to overcome any degree of spiritual blindness we encounter in this life, and to return to Father with an increased capacity to see.

Spiritual blindness does not occur all at once. It is a process that happens over time and according to our choices and depth of repentance. Similarly, improving our spiritual vision depends on our small acts of obedience and faith.

However, because our work is so vitally important, Satan isn't going to let us improve our spiritual vision without putting up a fight. We can expect his interference. In fact, we can count on it. How does he do this? He tries to persuade us to discount our role as God's children by making temptation and sin seem appealing and harmless.

Now, I know that not many of us are going to wake up and go commit murder, rob a bank, or some other major sin. It is more likely that we will give in to smaller temptations that will decrease our sensitivity to the Spirit and lead us away from Christ—even, perhaps, without our realization. But whether our sins seem large or small, they are still sins, and they stand as light-blockers.

If we let them, the normal, everyday emotions, attitudes, and behaviors we experience, although natural, can become obstacles to the Spirit.

We may be tempted to become and remain angry or resentful. We may give in to the feeling of not being enough and want to quit trying. Demands upon our energies may exhaust or discourage us, and we may not see the value of our efforts. Fear can overpower faith. Feelings of guilt, regret, or longing for the past can darken our present, and we are left without the vision we need to endure faithfully.

Remembering our role as Father's children can help us combat these and other everyday feelings and natural impulses so that our spiritual sight is not hampered. Remembering will help turn us to the Son. Light and power are available to each of us through the Atonement of Christ. No matter the situation we are in, no matter the darkness we experience, He offers us light to lead us through.

When my world went dark, every part of my life was altered. I felt as though I was on unstable ground as a mother, as a wife, as a person. The only thing that kept me moving forward and not giving up was remembering that I was in the hands of the Lord. I knew that I was a real daughter of a real God who loved me. This knowledge was the only thing that felt stable and unchanging during the most unsettling experience of my life. When I felt like giving up, I made an increased effort to turn to Christ, and He brought me to a better place emotionally, physically, and spiritually.

We have everything to gain from facing the Son. Every bit of effort we expend to do so is worth it. Christ's light can renew, encourage, comfort, warn, direct, forgive, and restore. As we turn to Him, He will show us how to fulfill our role as children of Heavenly Father. Christ's light will bring miracles into our lives. In fact, the Light will make miracles of our lives.

Chapter 2

FACE THE SON BY FOLLOWING PROMPTINGS

Light-Blocker: Loneliness

I had just applied shampoo to my hair when the piercing rings of the smoke alarm began. I wrapped up in a towel and ran to the kitchen with soapy hair, water dripping everywhere. The screaming alarm had ceased, but I was worried nevertheless.

"I heard the noise, Mommy," Benji, age five, said innocently as he met me in the kitchen. He reported that he had just been playing with toys and had heard the alarm. Hmm. Something seemed fishy, but I made no accusations. I instructed him to stay out of the kitchen. He went back into the playroom to resume his play and I returned to de-soap.

Well, a few minutes later, the alarm screams sounded once more. I again panicked. I wondered if my sweet

Smokey the Bear was playing camping again, as he had a few days earlier with some neighbor boys and some matches, or if the alarm was malfunctioning (one can always hope).

It took longer for the alarm to stop this time. Smokey explained that a box of matches had "fallen" out of the cupboard and one match had fallen out. That had made the alarm go off. I hate it when that happens.

Calmly, I asked my son to bring me the box and the match that had fallen out so unexpectedly—especially when I thought the matches were sufficiently hidden.

Later, the boys and I were in the playroom and I found a bunch of used matches behind the TV. There were also marshmallows stuck onto several of them. I'm not kidding!

"Benji, were you roasting marshmallows?"

The carpet was a bit melted in spots and there was ash on the floor. Let's hear it for indoor camping!

Man, was I grateful for smoke alarms that day. However, the warning system that I prefer is the Spirit of the Lord. The Spirit can send us messages of warning, as well as truth, knowledge, and comfort, but his method is much softer than a smoke alarm. In order to utilize this warning system, we must tune our hearts and minds to the voice of the Holy Ghost. This type of spiritual listening is a vital component of our spiritual eyesight. Clear as mud? Let me explain.

I'm frequently asked if, because of the loss of my

eyesight, my other senses are heightened. Remember the Bionic Woman? Well, that's pretty much me. All right, not really.

It's not that my other senses are automatically heightened, but my need to rely upon them is. My sense of touch and hearing both compensate for my inability to see. I have to depend upon these senses, perhaps more than other people, so they may be sharpened through use. The remaining senses I have work together to feed me information about my safety, my surroundings, and the people near me.

And so it is with our spiritual vision. We use our hearts, minds, and spiritual sensitivities to hear, see, and understand things of the Spirit. With this understanding, we will receive knowledge concerning our spiritual safety, hidden dangers in our surroundings, and the needs of the people near us.

As we develop these spiritual senses, it is vital to know how Father communicates with us individually so that we can act on the communications He has for us.

I have a good friend who loves to use his GPS in his car. You know the lovely voice that tells you constantly where to turn? "Turn right in 3.3 miles. Turn right in 2.2 miles. Turn right in 1.1 miles." Then, if you choose not to listen, it says, "Recalculating," and gives you a whole new set of instructions.

Well, my friend loves to set his GPS voice to the Frenchwoman setting. He loves to hear the beautiful female accent give him directions. Now, this may not seem out of the ordinary, but my friend doesn't speak French. So, his GPS may provide pleasant background noise, but it doesn't help much in the way of navigation.

Father in Heaven sends His communications in a way that we can understand. We just need to identify that way. In addition to studying the scriptures and talks from General Authorities on this topic, we can go to Father in prayer and ask how He talks to us. Then, as we are seeking light and remaining open to it, we will receive training in how we personally can recognize the Holy Ghost.

How do you hear the Spirit? If you are not sure, then now is the time to learn what language Father uses with you personally.

Once we can identify it, we can then obey. And hearing and obeying the Spirit will help us overcome another light-blocker—loneliness.

As a new mother, I had many days when I just felt lonely. There I was, totally responsible for this brand-new baby, feeling overwhelmed and unsure, with no adult to talk with me for hours. To add to my situation, because of my limited vision, I could not drive and had no way of going anywhere on my own. I felt stuck.

As I prayed for help, I was prompted to take my baby and visit the woman next door in our apartment complex. Leora was an older widow who was very lonely, and soon we became good friends. She loved holding Christopher and having someone to talk to. So did I.

I spent a lot of time helping her around her apartment, doing things that were difficult for her to do. I cleaned and vacuumed and took out her trash. And she held Christopher, which gave me a much-needed break. My new friend frequently joined our family for family home evening, and she taught me so many things about enduring cheerfully.

I realized that as I focused on Leora's needs, I wasn't as lonely and didn't feel so trapped. I started praying to know who else might be in need of a friend, and I was prompted to go to another apartment where two ladies in my ward lived. As baby Christopher and I visited this mother and daughter, I found two more friends who would help minimize the loneliness in my life.

Each day, I would ask Heavenly Father to lead me to those who might be in need of a friend. I tried to listen for the promptings of the Spirit and then to follow them. Looking back on those years, I have sweet and happy memories of time spent with my dear friends in that apartment complex—both young and old. I would not have such great memories and friends if Father hadn't led me to them through the voice of the Holy Ghost.

I still try to pray for direction in how to help those around me. Sometimes I just have a thought to call a woman in my ward to say hello. Sure, at times I've wondered if it was really the Spirit or only my own idea, but I've learned to just follow the thought. Most of the time, when I've visited or called someone just because I was thinking of them, I could tell that they appreciated my efforts. It may be scary to think of going out of your comfort zone, but stepping out of your loneliness to follow spiritual communications is well worth the little bit of discomfort.

Loneliness can become a dangerous light-blocker because when we're lonely we tend to look only to our own circumstances, and that can lead us to sadness, self-pity, discouragement, and so on. Loneliness, if we allow it, can start us on a spiral downward into darkness and away from the light. However, if we know how Heavenly Father speaks to us, and we ask for His promptings when we are lonely, we will not be left alone. Instead, we will find happiness outside ourselves, and that will help us move closer to the Son.

Chapter 3

FACE THE SON BY TRUSTING IN GOD'S PROMISES

Light-Blocker: Fear

In my early teenage years, I experienced real fear. I was on vacation with my family, and one of our daytime activities was to go rappelling off a cliff.

I watched the others rappel down the steep, rocky mountainside, and they all said it was so much fun. However, when it was my turn, I became paralyzed with fear. I looked out at the rocks below me and couldn't take the backwards step off the cliff. When, with much encouragement, I finally took that literal leap of faith, I began to cry. It wasn't fun at all. In fact, I thought I was going to die.

I was belayed to the guide at the top, and as I dangled in midair, I clung to the rope and cried up to him, "Pull me up! I can't do this! Pull me up!"

Little by little, I was talked down that mountainside—sobbing, but I made it to the solid earth below, and I did not die. I'm sure I made quite a sight.

Can you identify times in your life when you have been petrified with fear or worry? You might be experiencing such a time now. Life presents each of us with many situations when we can be overcome with fear for ourselves or for those we love.

In my case, rappelling seems like a piece of cake compared to what I've had to go through since then. When I was diagnosed with cancer, I was terrified that I would not survive, and when I did, I didn't want to. How would I function in the dark? How *could* I do it? How could I live my whole life blind when I was afraid just to take a few steps on my own? Would the cancer return?

I was consumed with fear—fear for myself and for my little family. How would I be able to care for my sons? Would I ever again be strong enough or able to be a good wife to my sweet husband? Would I ever be happy again?

It's impossible to describe the fear that continually gripped my heart and mind for over a year. I often found myself physically tense and on the defense for whatever horrible thing was going to happen next. Because I had been through five surgeries in about five months, battled cancer, and lost my sight, I just knew bad news was going to be around the next corner. Because I had been so deeply hurt by things over which I had no control, I lived in constant fear of what I would be dealt next.

I wish I could say that I had some miraculous experience, and all the fear immediately left, but that wasn't the case. It was a long, arduous journey, and my fear faded a bit at a time as I fought my way forward.

Looking back, three things stick out to me that helped me to overcome my fear. The first was time. I had been through a horrendous six months filled with trauma, and I needed to allow myself to feel all the feelings that came along with cancer, surgeries, blindness, loss, and change. I expected myself to handle things quickly, but that expectation was unrealistic. It takes time to move through pain and fear and to adapt to change, big or small.

Training was the second thing that reduced fear in my life. Although I was unwell for months following my surgeries, I forced myself to go each day for over five months to a training program that helped me adjust to being blind. I learned to read Braille, to use adaptive software on my computer, to cook, clean, and work around my house, and to navigate my way around using a white cane. Again, I had to be patient with myself, which was difficult, but with each new skill I mastered, I stepped a little further away from the fear.

The third and most important aid was to trust Heavenly Father. I had to believe that He knew what I was to become and what was required of me to get there. I trusted that He wouldn't leave me alone, and He never did. Even when I didn't feel His comfort or love, I know His love never ceased to surround me.

There seems to be a never-ending supply of things for each of us to fear or worry about. However, if we see life only through the darkening lens of fear's blur, then we are not fully living in the light of faith. Of course, we will be faced with fears throughout our lives, but we do not have to remain afraid.

When I was a little girl, in order to preserve my vision, I was given specific instructions from my eye doctor. Because of the radiation I had received as an infant, the blood vessels in my eyes were very brittle, and in order to prevent hemorrhaging, I was restricted from any physical activity that might shake or jar my head. My doctor would say, "Hold very still. Be as still as a china doll."

I think of his words when I consider the Lord's counsel, "Be still and know that I am God" (D&C 101:16). When I am incapacitated by fear, stress, or worry, I try to be emotionally and spiritually a china doll. If I take a deep breath and try to calm myself internally, I can then turn my thoughts to Father so that my spiritual sight can begin to clear.

Then I am able to "know that [He is] God." I can know Him, and you can know Him—His character, His love, and His promises.

Remembering God's promises has helped me be more filled with faith and more focused on the comfort of His light to lead me out of fear.

"I will not leave you comfortless" (John 14:18). This is a promise I rely on. In those times when I feel alone, fearful, and desperately in need of comfort, I call on the Father for this promise to be fulfilled. His comfort always comes. God does not break His promises—not ever.

Because Father in Heaven has helped me throughout my life, I knew that He would help me through the months of fear following my cancer and blindness, and He will help you. Whatever your fear, He will not leave you alone. His strength will come. It will. He will cast out the darkness of fear with His light-filled love. For He has promised, "I will . . . be your light in the wilderness; and I will prepare the way before you, if it so be that ye shall keep my commandments" (1 Nephi 17:13).

When we are confronted with fears about our children, spouses, jobs, money, future, health, and so forth, we can remember and trust that the Lord will send His assistance. We can rest in that promise.

Looking back on my rappelling experience, I realize that, although I was terrified and utterly sure I would die, I was actually safe, held secure by the guide above me. If I had placed more trust in him and listened to his directions, I would have actually enjoyed the experience. I would have realized that I had the capability to do such a difficult task.

And so it is with our lives. If we stay connected to the Lord and listen to His instructions and promptings, we will know and feel that we truly are in His hands. With His promised help, we have the capacity to do difficult things, and because of Him, we can see more clearly and need not remain afraid.

Chapter 4

FACE THE SON BY SEEKING TRUTH FROM THE SOURCE

Light-Blocker: Self-Criticism

A number of years ago, one of my friends was suffering from some health problems, and I would often drop by to help her with housework. On one particular day, I was cleaning her bathroom and ran into some trouble with the mirror. No matter how I tried to clean the glass, it remained hazy and blurry. At the time, I had poor vision, and I attributed the foggy mirror to that. However, on closer inspection, I found that my eyes were not at fault. I couldn't figure out the problem. I was using the bottle marked as glass cleaner, but I couldn't clean the glass. I was baffled.

Embarrassed by my failure to get the simple job done, I reported the trouble to my friend and apologized that her mirror still was not clean. It turned out that her husband had filled a bottle marked as glass cleaner with bleach. I was coating the glass with a layer of white film as I sprayed the bleach, and no amount of buffing cleared the foggy mirror.

I have thought a lot about that experience, and about my blurred image in that mirror. I wonder if, when we evaluate ourselves, we might not be seeing a clear image. What we may see and believe to be reality might actually be a distortion or stark untruth.

When you consider who you are, who do you see? What words do you use to describe yourself? Do you like who you are? Do you view yourself as having talents and gifts, or are you constantly criticizing or finding fault with yourself? It is so easy to fixate on the negative traits we possess and minimize or discount the good.

But constantly chiseling away at ourselves with criticism and negative talk does not bring happiness. Worse—it plays perfectly into Satan's plan for our misery. He would have us view ourselves as worthless, no good. This is not from Christ; therefore, it is darkness, and it will contribute to our spiritual blindness, for "that which doth not edify is not of God, and is darkness" (D&C 50:23).

Instead of seeing a glorious spirit child of the Almighty God, when Satan fogs the glass, we soon believe his distortions.

Perhaps we mistakenly believe that we are being humble

and that focusing on what is imperfect is a way to avoid pride. However, tearing ourselves down and looking for fault where there is really good is not humility. We would be much happier, and have more light in our lives, if we could break this damaging habit. But how do we do it?

First of all, we need to recognize the criticism and stop it. One of my friends yells, "Cancel!" when she notices that she is speaking negatively of herself. It stops her critical talk immediately, not to mention that it scares me every time.

Perhaps this strategy will work for you. Choose a word to say to stop your self-criticism. It can be any word: *spinach, diphthong, snicklefritz, lollipop*. Your friends may wonder why you all of a sudden yell, "Pickle!" or "Platypus!" while you are talking. You might just become the most talked-about woman in your neighborhood. Just tell your friends you aren't going crazy but are practicing a strategy to improve your vision.

It is true. As we learn to stop criticizing ourselves, our spiritual sight will improve. This happens because the negative words that bring darkness are removed from our automatic talk.

The next step is to think of and talk about ourselves with love, in a way Christ would approve. However, this may not be easy or comfortable because criticism has been a habit for so long. "Some of you may feel that you are not as attractive and beautiful and glamorous as you would like to be. Rise above any such feelings, cultivate the light you have within you, and it will shine through as a radiant expression that will be seen by others" (Gordon B. Hinckley, "The Light within You," 99).

Truthfully, we may not recognize the good within us or the strengths and talents we possess. We may need help in discovering the good and believing it.

There was a time in my life when my peers were critical, judgmental, and even rude about my physical appearance, and I was very hurt. I wondered if they were right. In order to avoid falling into the trap of feeling and thinking badly of myself, I sought truth about who I really was. Was there anything good about me?

The answers had to come from a source of truth and perfect knowledge. This source was the Father of my spirit. Who else would better know me? I studied my patriarchal blessing and was taught a few of the things my Father in Heaven gave me as strengths. I felt the truth of what I had learned, and this gave me power to resist believing the words of those around me who were critical.

Of course there was good inside me. There is good inside each of us. In fact, there is greatness within each of us. To find it, we must go to the source: our Father in Heaven. As I have done this, He has shown me glimpses of who I really am. By coming to know Him and His plan for me, I have come to better accept and love myself. This can be the case for each of us.

As we seek truth about ourselves, the Spirit can act as a mirror, providing a clear image, for "by the power of the Holy Ghost [we] may know the truth of all things" (Moroni 10:5). If we take our thoughts and feelings about ourselves to Heavenly Father, we can ask Him if there is any truth to them. He will answer. If we listen for and feel the promptings of the Holy Ghost, we will learn the truth or the error of our self-evaluations. We will learn where we need to improve, and we will see more clearly the good inside of us. Naturally, this includes putting our lives in alignment with Father's commandments so that we are worthy to receive spiritual knowledge from the Holy Ghost. Through this continual process, truth will be revealed to us, and we will be able to speak with love about ourselves.

We don't have to live in the fog of distortions fed to us by the enemy when we have access to personal, spiritual truth. It is that simple—not easy, but simple. As we are tutored by the Holy Ghost concerning our worth, talents, and strengths, we can follow the counsel of President Dieter F. Uchtdorf, "Don't let the voice of critics paralyze you—whether that voice comes from the outside or the inside" ("Happiness, Your Heritage," 119).

Chapter 5

FACE THE SON BY SEEKING JOY THROUGH GRATITUDE

Light-Blocker: Sadness

Some of my happiest childhood memories are the times I spent playing with my family. We played all sorts of games and enjoyed being together.

The game "Sardines" was one family favorite. To play this, all the lights were turned off and one family member hid somewhere in the house. After a few minutes had passed, another person would go in search of the first, and hide with him or her. This process would repeat until the whole family was squished together in one hiding place.

During one "Sardines" adventure, my older brother, Mark, hid first. His secret hiding place was the linen closet, which contained four shelves, each about seven feet long and two feet deep. One by one, we silently searched for

Mark, joining him in the closet when we found him. We tried our best not to laugh or make any noise as each new player struggled to find room among the mass of linens and bodies. By the time the game was finished, all eight of us were crammed into the closet, with several family members on each shelf.

We still laugh when we recall this particular "Sardines" night. We picture the sight we must have been all shoved tightly together, praying that the shelf above wouldn't collapse.

When we played this game, I loved huddling with my siblings and waiting for the next player, but I hated being the one to seek. It seemed to take such a long time to find the group in the dark, and I often grew frustrated and wanted to give up. Sometimes I would loudly whisper, "Tell me where you are. I can't find you." Then, those hidden would take pity on me and reveal their hiding place so that the game could continue.

Years later, I remembered my days of hide-and-seek games when I studied the words in the Relief Society Declaration. One phrase jumped out at me, and I smiled at the verbiage. As "beloved spirit daughters of God," we "*find* nobility in motherhood and joy in womanhood" (Mary Ellen Smoot, "Rejoice, Daughters of Zion," 92–93; emphasis added).

Isn't it interesting that we have to "find" our joy and nobility? This finding requires looking—even searching. Thankfully, when we face the Son, our search isn't solitary. We can have the companionship of the Spirit to assist us in finding joy.

Do you ever have those sad days when you wonder when you'll be happy? I do. There are times when I say to Heavenly Father, "Tell me where you are. I can't find you."

He does not seem so far away when I begin looking for His gifts and thank Him for them. Gratitude is a great remedy for sadness. It has the power to brighten and up-lift. Gratitude brings me closer to God. When I make a real effort to identify and show gratitude for even the smallest blessings I have, my spirit lifts, and I realize I'm not alone.

Being sad is part of mortality, and if you are like me, you've experienced plenty of sadness. Yet, joy and happiness are also part of this life. However, we may have to "find" them. We are practicing happiness here in preparation for our life with Christ. We practice as we seek moments of joy and then thank Father for them.

Can you recall any such moments? You might have felt a tugging at your heart when you saw your children playing nicely together, helping each other with chores, or showing compassion to someone in need. You might have celebrated with your son when he first realized that he had a testimony, or when your daughter helped you without being asked.

You might have felt grateful at work when a particular project was successful, or when someone noticed your expertise. That moment may have come with a visit from a grandchild or a note from a friend.

I have felt joy when my six-year-old cuddled up to me, saying, "This is my best day ever!" just because we jumped on the trampoline together. I have felt my heart smile when my ten-year-old son hugged me tightly and said he loved me. When Heavenly Father blesses me with a moment to teach my children a principle of the gospel, and they *get* it, that is a moment of joy for me. These are the times that help me remember that being a mother is worth all the struggles.

Our gratitude need not be limited to anything grand or profound. We can develop a habit of showing gratitude for even the most commonplace items, experiences, and interactions, especially in our darkest hours.

When sadness dims your vision, I urge you to add to an ongoing list of things and people you are grateful for. I am grateful for running water, lemon squares, the color green, comfy sweats, my bed, my ability to hear, rain, the ocean, Fudgesicles, my doggy, hot showers, microwaves, those little pellet ice cubes, fabric softener, old-fashioned doughnuts, and so much more. I am thankful for my darling, silly husband, the love of my brothers and sisters, the teaching and nurturing of good parents, the friendships I enjoy, and the gospel of Jesus Christ.

Gloom retreats when we make an effort to thank our Father for all we have. Our field of vision expands as we do this because our eyes are opened wide to the evidence of His love.

Chapter 6

FACE THE SON BY HOPING IN GOOD THINGS TO COME

Light-Blocker: Looking Backwards

After an hour, we finally arrived at our family reunion in a canyon near Salt Lake City, and I had one thing on my mind. I had to find the restroom.

Before we joined my husband's family members around the campfire, we detoured into the cabin. I opened the bathroom door, then closed and locked it. I leaned my cane in the corner and got all ready to sit on the toilet. You know how you do. However, as I was sitting down, I reached out my hand to find the toilet and felt instead . . . a head of hair! Needless to say, I yanked up my pants extremely quickly.

Noting the altitude of the head, I deduced that it was a

41

young head, and was probably a bit disturbed by what had flashed before its eyes. Talk about hindsight.

Trying to reassure my new friend, I inquired, "Was that scary?"

"Uh-huh."

It spoke! The head could speak! Why it hadn't found its voice earlier, I'm not sure, but I was glad to hear it nonetheless. After apologizing, I left my bathroom buddy and walked out to the group—shaking my head in disbelief. When they saw me approach, the family asked me what was wrong.

"I'll pay for therapy," I said. "Some little girl in the bathroom is going to need it."

You know, being able to look behind you does have its advantages.

I am amazed at the situations I get myself into. So many embarrassing things wouldn't happen if only I could see. As things stand, however, I guess I'll continue collecting experiences for my stand-up comedy routine.

But not all my experiences are funny. There have been times that have been so difficult and discouraging that I've longed to have my life back the way it was before my cancer and blindness. I miss the woman I used to be, the things I was able to do.

I look back to my days of light and wish things had

turned out differently. Do you, like me, ever suffer from the "if-only" syndrome? It is so easy to look to our past and say, "If only this or that hadn't happened, then . . . ," "Why didn't I . . . ?," or "Why did I . . . ?"

We can benefit by remembering lessons learned and good times we've had, but too much looking back can damage our spiritual eyesight. If we focus on mistakes, wallow in guilt or regret, hold tightly to grudges, or long for what has been lost, then our eyes are again removed from the Light. We are not facing the Son. Consequently, our vision dims, and our progression slows.

It may be extremely difficult to move beyond sadness, anger, or bitterness caused by past events. But if we remain stuck in those emotions, we forfeit light that can lead us forward. It works the same when we long for the good days of the past. We may not live fully in today because yesterday was easier or happier.

"I plead with you not to dwell on days now gone nor to yearn vainly for yesterdays, however good those yesterdays may have been. The past is to be learned from but not lived in. We look back to claim the embers from glowing experiences but not the ashes. And when we have learned what we need to learn and have brought with us the best that we have experienced, then we look ahead and remember that *faith is always pointed toward the future*. Faith always has to do with blessings and truths and events that will *yet* be efficacious in our lives" (Jeffrey R. Holland, "The Best Is Yet to Be," 24; emphasis in original).

I love the truth that faith points us and helps us to move forward. Faith in Jesus Christ promises hope for good things to come. It brings meaning to our struggles and offers courage for us to continue through dark times. Faith in Jesus Christ brings light.

My life is definitely not easy, and I don't like living every day in darkness. But my faith in my Savior leads me to have hope in what lies ahead.

I invite you to allow Christ to hold and heal pain from the past. Allow His sacrifice to pay for sin—your own and that of others who have hurt you. Point yourself forward with hope in a loving God who wants your happiness. This takes work, of course, but faith will bring the needed strength found through and in the Atonement.

Obtaining hope is a process. It may not come in a flash. But it is a spiritual gift that Father will endow us with as we seek it.

It's true that I miss those far-off days of light, but I know that the woman I was had not been polished enough to someday sit with my Savior and my Father. I needed to grow more. I needed to become more. Although I thought I would never again be happy after I went blind, my hope in Christ has brought me to a much better place—a place where joy still exists.

Whether our past is filled with sadness or joy, we cannot dwell there. This life is all about progression, and our individual growth will come as we keep our eyes firmly facing forward. We cannot look backward and move forward at the same time.

Have hope. There is joy and happiness ahead. There are good things to come.

Chapter 7

FACE THE SON BY TURNING COMPLAINTS INTO PRAYERS

Light-Blocker: Complaining

S craping ivy off the exterior wood of my house was not my idea of fun, but that is what my sister and I had to do for hours. It was a hot day in August, and for his birthday, my father decided that, as a family, we were going to stain the outside of our house. I had to help in the preparation by endlessly (it seemed) scraping walls. Yippee! What a fun birthday! More important, as a young girl, what an awful thing to have to do, and boy, did I complain.

Anyone who has tried to get children to clean their rooms, brush their teeth, do their homework, take out the trash, or any other form of work is familiar with the inevitable eruption of complaints. And whoever decided that "Saturday Is a Special Day" (*Children's Songbook*, 196) surely

46

never had children. It is my least favorite day of the week. Doing Saturday jobs about puts me over the edge as I try to teach my boys to work. It's a true miracle if I can make it through the morning without losing my cool.

Do any of these lovely expressions ring a bell?

"It's not my job!"

"Why do I have to clean up my room?"

"It's not fair that we have to do all the work! We're not your servants."

"I did it last time!"

And my favorite one, "Why don't you ever have to do any work, Mom?"

Ha! I get so tired of the "I don't want to . . ." and the "Why do I have to . . ." complaints.

Wouldn't it be blissful if, when we asked our children to do something, they would do it without complaining?

I wonder if Heavenly Father ever feels like that. Think about it. There are billions of His children here on the earth, and how many complaints do you think He hears— not just to Him, but about Him? Now, Father is perfect and full of charity. He loves us even when we complain, but I wonder if He is saddened when we complain about the "jobs" He gives us.

When you and I complain, we voluntarily impede the Spirit and the light it offers when we so desperately need it. Complaints about our lives, our children, our jobs, our bosses, our husbands, our Church callings, our neighbors, our bodies, and so forth, all blind us in some way. They stop us from progressing spiritually because we are focusing only on what is wrong. In this way, we aren't receiving light, but blocking it.

Do you and I ever complain about our trials? Do you ever feel guilty of thinking or saying things like, "I don't want to do this calling!" "Why did this have to happen right now?" "Why is my child this way?" "Why me?" "It's too hard!" "Do I have to?" "If God loved me, then why did He let this happen?"

Our frustrations about our difficulties and challenges are real, but if we do nothing but complain about them, then we are in opposition to Heavenly Father's will, and this brings only darkness. In this we will not be happy.

So, what do you and I do with our frustrations and complaints? Do we just smile and pretend everything is hunky-dory? No. There are many ways to turn our complaints to our benefit, enabling us to see more clearly.

One such way is demonstrated in 1 Nephi 16. Lehi and his family found themselves in a very precarious situation. Some of them were led to complain, even "murmur exceedingly, because of their sufferings and afflictions in the wilderness" (1 Nephi 16:20). At this time, Nephi had broken his bow, and his brother's bows had lost their springs, so they were unable to get food to provide for their families. Needless to say, they were all hungry and began to complain. Now, we might expect this from Laman and Lemuel, but even stalwart Lehi "began to murmur against the Lord his God" (v. 20).

I don't know about you, but when I need food, I get pretty grouchy. All other things seem to take a back seat until I am able to feed my body. Their situation is one I wouldn't sign up for. I can imagine the group of travelers all gathered around complaining about their hunger, blaming Nephi for their situation, and then blaming God.

Nephi's response and actions teach me a great lesson. He too was hungry, but instead of complaining against the Lord, he took action. He made a new bow and arrow out of the resources he had available to him. Then, he went to Lehi—his father and priesthood leader—for direction. After Lehi repented and humbled himself, the Lord instructed him where Nephi should go to find food. Nephi was obedient to this instruction and was able to bring home the much-needed nourishment for the group.

There is a pattern in this. When we are in difficult situations and are tempted to complain, even against the Lord, we too can make the choice to actively pursue a solution to the problem. We can use what we have available to us, seek help from family and priesthood leaders, and obey the word of the Lord and His prophets.

Additionally, we can use sincere prayer to help us access light and power during difficult times. When I was a child, my mother taught me a tool that can help you, like it does me, to conquer complaints. If we put the words "Dear Father in Heaven" in front of our feelings, and close in the name of Christ, then we have turned our frustrations and complaints into prayer. This is a much more positive way to express ourselves. We are opening our hearts to heaven for help instead of hardening our hearts against Father's will.

The technique of turning my complaints into prayers helped me through some of the toughest months I've ever endured. When I lost my vision, and my body was so unwell during my recovery process, you can bet I had plenty of complaints. I was absolutely miserable every second that I was awake. Day after day, sometimes even minute after minute, I pled with my Father in Heaven to help me through the horrible pain—both physical and emotional. "I don't want to be blind, Heavenly Father. Please help me." "I'm too weak to take care of my children. I need help." "Please help me find something to smile about today." "I can't do this anymore!" "Please help me through this pain."

As I took my complaints to him, Father sent the calming spirit of the Holy Ghost to reassure me that I was heard.

My desperate prayers, filled with my concerns and complaints, over time assisted me through the anger and misery to a much more stable place. The problems didn't all evaporate, but I grew stronger and my heart became softer.

Turning our complaints heavenward works with large, traumatic situations as well as our day-to-day gripes. When you and I are at work, at home, in the car, shopping, or interacting with our families, and we catch ourselves complaining out loud or in our minds, we can stop, turn these thoughts to God, and actually receive help to deal with the things or people we're complaining about. When we do this, we allow the light and knowledge of heaven into our hearts and minds. It is easier to accept Father's will when we ask to know it instead of complaining about it.

Sound too simplistic? Try it for yourself. I think you'll find, as I have, that through this process, you will complain less, feel the Spirit more, and feel better and happier about your life.

Chapter 8

FACE THE SON BY LISTENING TO THE WORDS OF LIVING PROPHETS

Light-Blocker: Discouragement

Recently, I felt like going for a walk in the fresh air, so I grabbed my white cane and began my adventure. As I made my way along the sidewalk in my neighborhood, my face was abruptly introduced to an overgrown prickly tree. Of course, after yelling, "Ouch!" quite loudly, I stopped, muttered something about people needing to cut back their trees, and then made my way around the barricade blocking my path. I think, from now on, when I go out walking, I may need to wear a helmet and carry clippers.

After crossing a busy street, I had several other small mishaps and grew discouraged. I wondered why just going for a walk had to be such hard work. It would be much easier, not to mention much less painful, if I just stayed at home.

I had similar but more intense feelings of discouragement on another occasion as I began making homemade wheat bread. I put the wheat in the wheat grinder, turned it on, and waited for it to do its job. When I checked inside for the flour, the container was empty. I then realized that I had not put the lid to the grinder on correctly. Instead of collecting in the appropriate container beneath the grinder, the flour had spewed forth and now covered everything in my kitchen—including me. Standing in the middle of my indoor Winter Wonderland, I exclaimed, "You've got to be kidding me!"

I then commenced the disaster cleanup. I cleaned and cleaned until I had restored the kitchen to its pre-flour decor. Well, at least I thought so, until my husband came home and gasped, "What exploded in our kitchen?" There was still more flour—on top of the fridge, coating the walls and cupboards, and decorating all kitchen appliances. Sure, the bread recipe was easy, but the entire experience proved more than I had bargained for.

Sometimes, living in the dark can be very discouraging. Tasks that seem so simple can require more effort than I feel I can put forth. However, I will continue going for walks, and I will dare to make bread again.

With or without vision, life can be very discouraging. At times, we may conclude that it would be so much easier just to give up. It is crucial to realize that discouragement is an effective power tool of Satan. He wants us to become overwhelmed and upset. He wants us to give up.

If the devil can persuade us to give in to discouragement, we are likely to remain in the darkness of despair. It's only when we face the Son, when we turn our eyes to the Light, that we will see our situation clearly.

Discouragement can come from so many angles. We may feel it when our fashionable, form-fitting jeans are replaced by the dreaded fat pants, or when we don't recognize the woman staring back in the mirror (that is, if you can see the mirror). Feelings of frustration and discouragement may set in after a long day's labor to clean the house, only to have the family walk in and trash it in two seconds flat. You may be completely discouraged in dating, wondering where your future spouse may be. Or you may have been married for years and are wondering where you can send your spouse.

Perhaps you have felt discouraged concerning the decisions of a child. Juggling work, family, and home may become so overwhelming that you may feel like you're drowning in all life's demands. You may be frustrated because all of the work of raising a family is on your shoulders.

Discouragement's darkness comes to all of us, but, having also suffered with depression, I know the darkness that runs deeper and lasts longer than seems bearable. Sometimes light can seem completely blotted out by the hopelessness of clinical depression, and you may wonder if you'll ever make it out of the darkness. If you feel this way, don't give up! Don't give in to despair! There is help available to you through competent professionals and those who love you.

Having depression doesn't mean you are less faithful than anyone else. It is a condition that comes to some because of mortality. You may not be able to pray it away. Nor will fasting or more reading of the scriptures erase the disorder. These habits will, of course, help you gain strength and lead you closer to the Lord, but not all suffering can be removed even if we are faithful. Nor should it be. Hold onto Christ, for He has already suffered what you are suffering. He will help you through this and lead you to those who can help. Others may not understand depression, but He understands completely.

On the other hand, most people are familiar with the darkness that comes with temporary discouragement. Not only am I familiar with it, but I feel like it was a houseguest throughout 2004 as I tried to pick up my life after my cancer. One experience in particular stands out in my mind as overwhelmingly discouraging. Smack! I walked right into the wall. It had only been a few weeks since I had gone blind, and I, naturally, had not seen the wall on my way to the bathroom in the middle of the night. In my blunder, I had hit my face, already hurting from surgery, and I began to cry silently, "I don't want to be blind anymore!"

Right there, in my physical and emotional darkness, I wondered how I would ever make it. Where would I ever gain the strength to endure one more day of blindness—let alone a lifetime?

My physical and emotional improvement seemed non-existent, and every day I wondered if I would ever be happy again.

During these difficult days, weeks, and months, I listened to my scriptures on audio recordings as well as talks from the prophets and other General Authorities of the Church. These messages sparked my resolve to press forward and served as a much-needed light.

When I needed extra strength to face yet another surgery, the Spirit touched me deeply through a message by Elder Jeffrey R. Holland. He taught that true dedication and discipleship to Jesus Christ is not always convenient. If we sincerely want to be Christ's, and wish to dwell with Him eternally, then we must be willing to partake of a bitter cup, as He did, and remain faithful. For, "The cup and the throne [are] inextricably linked and [can] not be given separately."

Elder Holland further asked us to ask ourselves, "If we are Christ's and he is ours, are we willing to stand firm forever? Are we in this church for keeps, for the duration, until it's over? Are we in it through the bitter cup, the bloody baptism, and all?" (*On Earth as It Is in Heaven*, 155).

My cup was definitely bitter, yet I knew that remaining a faithful disciple was the only way to make it through my pain and out of the discouraging darkness that engulfed me. I had to stay the course until eventually I could return to Him.

Years have passed since that time of deep discouragement, but my trials are not over, and neither are those times when I become disheartened and want to give up. When I feel discouragement creeping into my heart, I still turn to the words of the Lord's chosen servants. I listen to general conference addresses and college devotionals by Church leaders. Instead of blasting my music—which I still do at times—while cleaning, making dinner, or folding laundry, I turn up the volume on my computer and soak up the Spirit and truth from their online messages. Doing this has allowed the Comforter to buoy and encourage my troubled mind, and I have found solace in the Spirit while performing even the most mundane tasks.

Perhaps you enjoy reading the printed messages more than listening to audio recordings, but either way, the teachings of the modern-day prophets and apostles can, with the light of truth, help burn away the suffocating haze of discouragement.

You and I are loved infinitely. As evidence of this love, Father has sent us holy prophets and apostles to fill us with hope and lift us up. When we seek comfort through their words, we will find light and courage to continue forward— even if it's just to go for a walk or make bread.

Chapter 9

FACE THE SON BY LIVING VERTICALLY

Light-Blocker: Comparison

"Chia Head." That's what my little brothers called me years ago when I had to have my head shaved prior to a brain surgery. As my hair grew back, they thought I resembled a Chia Pet—you know, one of those animal-shaped terra-cotta planters that sprouts. Ha-ha! They thought they were so funny.

The thing was that only the top half of my head had to be shorn, leaving my hair nearly shoulder length in the back. So I'm sure I actually looked like a Gadianton robber. Truthfully, I felt more than ugly. I was surprised how much my hair was connected to my self-concept. I did not want to wear a wig, and therefore spent a few months wearing hats until my hair had grown out and no longer resembled Velcro.

I was extremely self-conscious and wished for my hair. Everyone around me had hair—even cute hair. And mine? Talk about a "bad hair day."

I began to compare not only my hair with others', but my life as well. No one else around me needed brain surgery, had eye problems, or had physical restrictions on their activities.

Comparison is such an easy trap to fall into. Almost without realizing it, we may often measure ourselves by what others can do, what they wear, how much money they seem to have, the size of their house, the size of their waist, how talented they are, and on and on. It's interesting that it is usually our weaknesses that we compare to others' strengths. We set ourselves up for a pretty good pity party. And you know what happens then. The light and love from the Spirit is blocked by the darkness of self-pity, jealousy, pride, and envy. If we nourish these light-blocking feelings, we eventually may even be tempted to criticize others or gossip about them.

Sister Bonnie Parkin has stated it this way, "We . . . lose sight of that good part when we compare ourselves to others. Her hair is cuter, my legs are fatter, her children are more talented, or her garden's more productive—sisters, you know the drill. We just can't do that. We cannot allow ourselves to feel inadequate by focusing on who we *aren't* instead of on who we are! We are *all* sisters in Relief Society. We simply cannot criticize, gossip, or judge *and* keep the pure love of Christ" ("Choosing Charity: That Good Part," 105; emphasis in original).

There is a way to live that will bring us light, such that comparison's darkness will be burned away. This light comes through what my mother calls "vertical living." Alma taught Helaman how to live this way when he said, "See that ye look to God and live" (Alma 37:47). I like to turn this phrase around so that it reads, "live—looking to God." It is a way of life.

This means that we focus upward—vertically—to Christ. Instead of comparing ourselves to those around us— horizontal to us—we look up in our thoughts.

Let me demonstrate how this works. I have a close friend who has an absolutely gorgeous singing voice. I don't mean she sounds good singing a solo part in the ward choir at the annual Christmas ham feast. I mean, this girl can sing. She writes beautiful, inspiring music and performs it, records it, and has helped thousands through sharing it.

Now, I would love to have her talents, but I do not. What I do have, however, is a choice. I can live in envy and jealousy, continually putting myself down for not being able to sing as well as my friend, until I convince myself that I have no talents whatsoever. Or, I can sincerely appreciate her talents, and then I can say, "Heavenly Father, I can't sing as well as I'd like, but I am grateful for the talent I have of . . . [fill in the blank here, for example: being a pretty good listener, cleaner, or writer]. What I have and can do, I give to thee." I then work on doing this.

If I need help identifying my talents or gifts, I can pray for that help and begin working to find them. Every time I am tempted to compare myself with my friend, or with anyone else, for that matter, I try to remember to focus my thoughts upward, to face the Son—to live vertically.

There is power in this. When I look or compare horizontally, or to those around me, the light is not visible to my envying and discouraged spirit; however, when I live vertically, I can see the light urging me to become my best self.

There is so much more that can be revealed to us as we try to stay focused upward. If we live vertically, we will see in ourselves what our Father wishes us to see.

My Chia Head days are in the distant past, but it's still easy to compare. I still have limitations and things I just can't do, but I try to focus on those things that I can do— and then do them to and for the Lord. You can do the same. Just live vertically. "Look to God and live" (Alma 37:47).

Chapter 10

FACE THE SON BY LOOKING ON THE HEART

Light-Blocker: Judging

One day, as her moral support, I accompanied my friend Josephine when she went to get her blood drawn at the hospital. When we entered the lab, Josephine bravely took her seat in the chair with the armrests near the phlebotomist, and I sat beside her to offer encouragement in facing the needle. However, the phlebotomist was dumbfounded, thinking we had made a mistake. She tried to get us to change seats so that she could take my blood.

Because I look blind and was holding onto Josephine's arm as we walked, I was the one who appeared to have the medical needs. The lab worker expected me to take the hot seat. Josephine would have been more than happy to allow me to take her place, but we explained to this confused woman that Josephine indeed was the correct patient.

I thought it was great that, for once, I wasn't the one to need the test.

This experience has been the catalyst for several discussions with friends about judging. Just as the woman at the lab assumed I was the patient, we may all be a little guilty of judging others based on their outward appearance. Although it may be natural, this way of judging may cause an astigmatism in our spiritual sight. In order to change, we will need corrective lenses provided by the Savior.

Since we are striving to become as Christ, we would be wise to learn and then emulate how He judges. In First Samuel, we are taught, "Look not on his countenance, or on the height of his stature . . . : for the Lord seeth not as man seeth; for man looketh on the outward appearance, but the Lord looketh on the heart" (1 Samuel 16:7).

Throughout my years of enduring rude comments and the stares of others, the truth found in this verse has always been special to me. No matter what, I know that the Lord sees my heart. He sees my intentions, hopes, joys, and desires.

How can you and I have such spiritual vision? The key is Jesus Christ. As we hold up the light, "which light is the light of Christ" (Moroni 7:18), we will be enabled to see the true nature of things, places, and people.

If we sincerely plead to the Father for help to look on the hearts of those around us, the light that comes from Christ will make that possible. We will be given insights and promptings we would receive in no other way. We can ask for and work to develop a spiritual gift—a depth of perception that we have not known before.

I experienced this personally many years ago in my own life. A sister in my ward whom I didn't know very well was given a particular calling, and I, frankly, wondered why. She didn't seem to fit the position. Had the bishop gotten the right woman? Was he really inspired on this one? Why hadn't he called someone else—someone like . . . me?

I raised my arm to sustain her, but I had some work to do within my heart in order to really do this. I prayed for quite some time to feel more charity for her. I asked Father to open my eyes to her strengths and good qualities. As I watched her serve, something miraculous happened. I grew not only to love this woman as a sister in the gospel but to love her as a friend. She was exactly right for the calling at that time in our ward. She was fun, thoughtful, loving, and sensitive to the Spirit. She truly loved and cared for those she served, including me.

With light given me through the Spirit, my judgmental

heart had softened and my spiritual sight had improved. Because I was willing to give up my prejudice, and because I prayed for charity, I was blessed with a witness of her calling. In fact, I was blessed with a dear friend.

Each of us can have experiences like this. Our attitudes and unrighteous judgments can be changed through contact with spiritual light. Our sight won't improve all at once, but I know that as we grow closer and closer to Jesus, our vision will become more like His. Our spirits will grow to be more in tune with the spirits of those around us, and, with an increased depth of perception, we will begin to look "on the heart."

Chapter 11

FACE THE SON BY SEEKING THE SPIRITUAL GIFT OF DISCERNMENT

Light-Blocker: Irritation

When I was a teenager, I treasured Saturday mornings. I couldn't wait for the weekend so that I could sleep in. The alarm clock was not set, I didn't have to go to early-morning seminary, and, for one precious day, I could stay in my comfy bed and sleep. That is, unless Dad came through the hall loudly singing the BYU Cougar Fight Song to wake us all up to do yard work.

Another irritating Saturday morning sleep disturber was the woodpecker who regularly dropped by for its morning feast. The stupid bird would jackhammer its little beak into the wood right outside my bedroom window, and it seemed like the incessant pecking bored into my skull. I would pound on the wall with my fist to scare the woodpecker away, and for a few minutes, it worked. Then, just as I fell back to sleep, the tap-tap-tapping would begin again. It was so irritating! Was it too much to ask for a little uninterrupted sleep?

As a mother, I am often reminded of that darn woodpecker when my children jackhammer me with questions, needs, and demands. In addition, their constant pestering of and quarreling with each other can be more than I can take. When one single afternoon feels like forever, eternity seems a little less appealing.

But this is a "natural man" reaction. When I let my vision be filled with the faults and bothersome behaviors of others, heaven's light is again obscured. I can become so bugged that the Spirit departs, and so does my happiness, as my irritation grows to anger. However, there is a higher way to live—a happier way.

In 2 Nephi 2:14, we learn from the words of Lehi that when God created the heavens and the earth, and all the things that were in them, He created "both things to act and things to be acted upon." You and I have been given the ability and freedom to act for ourselves. I can choose how to feel; I don't have to simply react to others and therefore be "acted upon."

However, just knowing that I have the agency to choose

does not eliminate the real irritation I feel. I need a tool to assist me in this change.

There is a spiritual gift available to you and me, which the Father will give us as we seek it. This is the spiritual gift of discernment. Elder David A. Bednar has taught: "The gift of discernment opens to us vistas that stretch far beyond what can be seen with natural eyes or heard with natural ears. Discerning is seeing with spiritual eyes and feeling with the heart—seeing and feeling the falsehood of an idea or the goodness in another person. Discerning is hearing with spiritual ears and feeling with the heart—hearing and feeling the unspoken concern in a statement or the truthfulness of a testimony or doctrine" ("Quick to Observe," 36).

Elder Bednar further explains that the gift of discernment allows us to see the hidden evil influences in others and in ourselves. It will also help us discover the concealed good in others and the good in ourselves.

Isn't this a fabulous blessing? We can be warned of the malicious intentions of others as well as perceive their goodness, either of which may be difficult to see. However, when we seek for this gift, we must be ready to look in the mirror placed before us to see both the good and error we also possess.

During a time when I really needed the light of heaven to assist me, I decided to put Elder Bednar's teachings to the test. I wanted to see how this spiritual gift of discernment could help me avoid becoming or remaining irritated. I pled in prayer to receive the gift of discernment concerning one of my sons. It is so easy to focus on his faults and shortcomings, and to overlook or not really see his goodness and correct behaviors. I can so easily let myself become irritated with how he acts. But this is not the kind of mother I wish to be. I want to *want* to be around my children. I want to see and celebrate their greatness.

An interesting thing began to happen as I prayed for and sought the spiritual gift of discernment. My son's good qualities were literally easier to see. I was able to feel his goodness, and his irritating behaviors didn't seem to bother me as much. At first, he didn't change, but I did. However, as I emphasized his goodness, he began to behave more appropriately and less annoyingly.

Another change occurred as well. I focused more on my faults than on his. As I tried to work on myself, I didn't spend that time noticing his behaviors, which had bothered me previously. When I focused on the "beam" that was in my own eye, I didn't spend my energy being bothered with the "mote" that was in his eye (see Matthew 7:3).

My experiment worked! It was wonderful to see how the words of an Apostle were demonstrated in my own life. However, when I stopped *striving* to receive this gift, I saw myself slide right back into the habit of being irritated. Keeping the spiritual gift of discernment requires constant work and prayer.

We can find many reasons to become irritated with others. But this is not what we are shown by the Light. Although the actions and habits of others may be worthy of irritation, we need not fall into the trap and be acted upon. We can act for ourselves according to the light we are given. You and I can petition the Father for the gift of discernment and see the hidden good in those around us. As we work to incorporate this gift into our character, we can avoid serious spiritual blindness and feel more joy in life.

Chapter 12

FACE THE SON BY CHOOSING NOT TO BE OFFENDED

Light-Blocker: Anger

When I was young, I dreamed of marrying Pahoran. You know, Pahoran, the chief judge in the book of Alma? Yes, I know he died hundreds of years ago, but I just loved him. I wanted to find a man with a heart like his.

If you remember, in the last chapters of Alma, the Nephites were in a very dangerous position, fighting yet again for their lives. The Lamanites and the king-men—Nephite dissenters—were overpowering the Nephites, and the freedom of the Nephite nation and their very lives were hanging in the balance. Captain Moroni had received a letter from Helaman describing the terrible circumstances he and his men were in, and Moroni then wrote a letter to the chief judge, Pahoran, in the capital city, demanding to know why he hadn't sent needed food and soldiers to assist Helaman.

Now, if I were Pahoran and had received Moroni's letter, I would have been severely hurt and angry—even outraged at the things he wrote. After all, although Moroni's intent was righteous, he had no idea what was really going on in the capital city of Zarahemla.

Pahoran had been true to the cause of freedom and had been chased out of Zarahemla by the enemy. He was gathering troops to go against the Lamanites. But Moroni, who did not know this, charged him with neglect.

Pahoran did not deserve these accusations, and he could have retaliated out of self-defense. He could have said things like: "How dare you accuse me of 'slothfulness'? We're risking our lives to defend this people, and you're calling us 'traitors to [our] country'?" (Alma 60:14, 18). But he didn't respond that way.

After Moroni wrote, "except ye do administer unto our relief, behold, I come unto you . . . and smite you with the sword" (Alma 60:30), Pahoran could have said, "You know, Moroni, we used to be friends, but after what you've said, I'm never speaking to you again! You can just deal with this war on your own, you ungrateful jerk. And by the way, remember that breastplate I loaned you? I want it back!"

Yet, again, he did not react like this. Pahoran chose not to become offended. His response was simply, "And now, in your epistle you have censured me, but it mattereth not; I am not angry, but do rejoice in the greatness of your heart" (Alma 61:9).

This Christlike reply is amazing to me! Pahoron even called Moroni "my beloved brother" (Alma 61:14) and said how much joy it gave him to receive his letter. I'm pretty sure this would not have been my initial response to such cutting words. But Pahoran knew this truth: "To be offended is a *choice* we make; it is not a *condition* inflicted or imposed upon us by someone or something else" (David A. Bednar, "And Nothing Shall Offend Them," 90; emphasis in original).

Pahoran knew Moroni's heart and rejoiced in his goodness. It must have been an answer to his prayers to know that Moroni was so dedicated to the freedom of his people that he would come to Pahoran's aid. Pahoran, however, did admit that he was hurt, even "censured"—deeply cut or wounded—by Moroni's harsh words. So, how did he get over the hurt and not become angry and bitter toward Moroni?

I am reminded of an experience I had a number of years ago, when I had been hurt deeply by a friend. I had been treated unfairly and, in my opinion, judged unrighteously.

My hurt grew to anger and festered inside of me. I couldn't even be around this person without fuming. I didn't like the way I felt, even though I knew I was justified in feeling mistreated.

Pahoran's response to Moroni served as a pattern for me at this time. I didn't want to harbor bad feelings or to carry around the anger. I wanted my heart to really feel like Pahoran's when he said, "It mattereth not" (Alma 61:9). But it was so difficult.

I prayed to have the Atonement of my Savior work in my life. I pled for love for this person and for the anger to dissipate. I even anonymously served her so that my heart would soften. I also went to this person, explained that I had harbored bad feelings toward her, and asked for forgiveness. Over time, the Spirit helped remove the hurt and anger.

What a dangerous light-blocker anger is! It seems to grow and spread until it consumes our thoughts and feelings. It may start with hurt and grow from anger to bitterness and, eventually, even possibly to rebellion against God. Society supports us in our anger, saying that our feelings are justified and retribution is deserved. However, as followers of Jesus Christ, we know that there is a higher way to live. For the "eye for an eye" practice only results in further blindness. And trust me: it's not all it's cracked up to be.

Christ has taught, "For inasmuch as ye do it unto the least of these, ye do it unto me" (D&C 42:38). We feel great about this scripture when we serve someone in need, but it is also true when we feel or show anger toward another. If we are angry with someone, it is vital to our spiritual growth and vision to remove the anger from our hearts so that we do not remain in opposition to Christ.

You and I interact daily with others, and we have many opportunities to become hurt and angry. We may be mistreated by a neighbor or ward member, betrayed or abandoned by someone we've trusted, or hurt by the words of a spouse or child.

There will always be occasions to become offended and hurt, but if we surrender to these feelings, as Pahoran could have, we will miss out on the joy that comes from forgiveness. Anger not only blocks out light but smothers it.

However, simply deciding not to be angry does not automatically remove the hurt and anger we feel. Along with work on our part, conscious choices not to take offense, and sometimes the passage of time, it takes the light of the Atonement to break through the dark cloud of anger. Clear vision comes when we remember that Jesus Christ gave His life—not just for us, but even for those who have angered or hurt us. Through the power of His Atonement, we can literally feel love for our wrongdoers. Our heavy hearts can become lighter as we invite and allow the Spirit to change us. This doesn't necessarily happen suddenly, but in the Lord's time, it will come.

Pahoran knew this truth. It enabled him to forgive and love Moroni. Similarly, you and I can personally come to know that it is only through the Atonement of Jesus Christ that our hurts can be healed, our anger can be removed, and our hearts can be filled with charity. When we are hurt, we can, with the help of Christ, obtain increased spiritual vision, so we can say, as Pahoran did, "But it mattereth not" (Alma 61:9).

Chapter 13

FACE THE SON BY RECEIVING HELP

Light-Blocker: Pride

I recently met a sweet woman who shared with me some of her struggles. She lives each day in chronic pain, and as we talked, I sensed she felt very burdened. She didn't have the physical strength to care for her children and run a household. In addition, she was single and had to work. My heart went out to my new friend, who was obviously overwhelmed and discouraged.

I asked if she had family nearby or if she had help from her neighbors or ward family. Sadly, she explained that many people had offered to assist her, but that she had refused their help. She thought it meant she was weak, or not being self-sufficient, if she accepted assistance from others, even though she needed it desperately.

Have you ever had such feelings? I have. I wonder if we might all, at some time, pray for help but then not want to accept it when assistance is offered by those around us. Have you, like me, ever answered, "No, I'm fine," when someone wants to help?

Although these feelings might be natural, on closer inspection, we might see that this kind of response actually blocks out light and further blinds us spiritually. If I believe I can handle problems completely on my own, I will miss out on the light that comes through living Heavenly Father's plan for His children—living as a family.

Refusing the help of those around us could be compared to my experience with cancer and fading vision. I had a life-threatening disease, and I would have been unwise to have refused the help of the doctors. If I had said, "No, I can handle it on my own. I don't need your help," where would I be now? I would be not only blind but dead. When we refuse the help of others, are we doing a similar thing spiritually?

I spoke once with a loved one who was going through some serious difficulties. I had been prompted to tell him that I was there for him if he needed a listening ear. Immediately, he went on the defensive and refused my offer. He stated emphatically that throughout his whole life, he hadn't needed anyone's help. When he had problems, he took them to the Lord, and that was all he needed to do.

He was on the right track, but I believe he was missing out on further light that was available. Taking our troubles to our Father is exactly what we should do, but that is not the end of the process. As President Spencer W. Kimball taught, "The Lord does notice us, and he watches over us. But it is usually through another person that he meets our needs. Therefore, it is vital that we serve each other" ("President Kimball Speaks Out on Service to Others," 47).

This is the design of our Father. We need each other. Of course, we need to do what we can for ourselves and not rely solely on the help of others, remaining dependent and helpless. But if Father in Heaven had wanted us to handle every trial on our own, without assistance from our brothers and sisters, He would have placed us each on our own planet. Although that may sound appealing at times, it is not the will of our Father that we cut ourselves off from the help of others.

Why is it so hard to accept help? Why would we rather serve than be served? Why don't we want others to see us as less than perfect? Could it be a case of pride? We may not want to admit it, but that is exactly what it is. Thinking most about how we might appear to those around us means that we have taken our eyes off of the light and focused on ourselves. Our vision dims due to our pride.

We may feel like we have to appear stronger than we

really are. We may confuse being self-sufficient with needing to handle all things absolutely by ourselves. We may view offers of assistance as threats to our abilities or even to our faith.

When others try to help, we may act a little like the puffer fish that, in order to defend himself from predators, inflates his body to appear larger than he really is. The predators then find that what looked like a small fish has suddenly changed, and they are often frightened away. Do we feel it important to protect our own pride by pushing others and their kindness away?

I think about the puffer fish and pride when I read the teachings of Mormon. Charity "is not puffed up" and "seeketh not her own" (Moroni 7:45). If I want to rid myself of pride, I can't remain "puffed up" as the puffer fish. Nor can I rely solely on or seek my own strength, my own power, or my own knowledge. I can learn to live a higher way.

Father's plan for His family is much wiser and brighter than our ideas of self-containment. He has given us a key to overcoming the darkness of pride. Mormon further teaches, "Wherefore, my beloved brethren, pray unto the Father with all the energy of heart, that ye may be filled with this love, which he hath bestowed upon all who are true followers of his Son" (Moroni 7:48).

As we pray for this spiritual gift of charity and begin to

feel the love of God, and to love like God, our hearts will recognize the love being extended to us. It will become easier to accept service because we will see it for what it really is—a manifestation of the love of our Father in Heaven.

This occurred in my own life a number of years ago. I had been hospitalized after being diagnosed with bacterial meningitis. This infection had caused tremendous pain, and I had been in a coma for four days. The doctors gave me little chance of survival, and they told my husband that if I did live, I would be a vegetable.

However, my life was preserved and my brain was miraculously undamaged. (*Well, that depends on who you ask.*) When I recovered sufficiently to be discharged, I returned home to the loving care of my family, as well as to an angel army of caring Relief Society sisters. These sisters—some of whom I hadn't met before—literally rescued me. Some cared for my sons, brought in meals, cleaned my house, did my laundry, and went grocery shopping. Others came in periodically to assist me in getting pain medications, and others came just to chat and keep me company.

Every now and then I would get a phone call from a sister who would say, "Hello, Kris, my name is So-and-so from the Relief Society. I haven't met you yet, but I'll be right over to make you lunch. Does anything sound good?"

Sure, I could have told these sisters that their service

wasn't necessary, or that my little family would handle it fine on our own. But I knew that their help was actually the answer to my pleadings to Heavenly Father to help me through this horrible experience.

It wasn't always comfortable to be cared for by women whom I barely knew, but I am so grateful I accepted their kindness. These sisters have become some of my closest friends. Through their love and service, and my acceptance of their assistance, I witnessed our hearts being "knit together in unity and in love" (Mosiah 18:21).

Father loves each of us perfectly, and He wants us not only to extend but to receive love, compassion, and service from our brothers and sisters on this earth. It may not come naturally, but through fervent prayer and sincere practice, we can become better at this important part of Father's plan.

By simply saying "thank you," being sincerely grateful for the love extended to us through service, we will begin to feel more light. Why? Because we are letting go of the darkness of pride.

It's all right to need help. It's okay to let others serve us, and even to ask for assistance. Doing this will improve our vision and bring us nearer to Jesus Christ—His love, His compassion, and His light.

Chapter 14

FACE THE SON BY USING WISDOM

Light-Blocker: Exhaustion

One week, about two years after I lost my vision, I was exhausted from all the demands placed on me. Every time I turned around, I was either cleaning up after Benji, my two-year-old, who got up an average of five times a night, or trying unsuccessfully to reason with Christopher, my six-year-old. I remember speaking with a doctor on the telephone regarding Benji's non-sleeping habits, and when I got off the phone, I found my dear toddler in the living room redecorating. He was playing Bob the Builder as he smashed the glass bulb ornaments on the Christmas tree with his plastic hammer. "Can we [break] it? Yes we can!" He was so proud. Ugh!

I began picking up the broken pieces of glass by Braille,

and, of course, I cut myself. After administering first aid and collecting all the large pieces of glass, I got out the vacuum to finish the job. However, Christopher had left his backpack on the floor, and I, not seeing it, vacuumed up the strap, which caused the vacuum belt to break and the motor to smoke. I then called my sweet neighbor and pled for assistance.

When the redecorating project was cleaned up, I found Benji in the kitchen, independently making a sandwich. That would have been a great accomplishment if he hadn't dumped an entire bottle of black pepper, garlic salt, and who knows what else between two slices of bread.

"I'm makin' a sammich, Mommy!" The contents of my spice cupboard were everywhere.

Again, I began the cleanup.

I was so disgusted with having to act as a human dustpan that I didn't notice that my son the whirlwind had gone on to his next adventure. This included using a permanent marker and some Monistat to create a lovely mural in my bathroom. His art was embellished with a whole package of eye patches, which he thought were stickers. The day was rounded out with Benji experimenting with putting objects in the toilet.

My week progressed with a similar theme.

Christopher came home from school on a snowy

afternoon, and he walked straight through the house and out the back door. For some reason, I followed him, and when I opened the door, I couldn't believe my ears.

"What are you doing, Christopher?" I asked calmly.

"I'm makin' yellow snow. But don't worry, Mom. I won't eat it."

We then had a discussion about the proper means of personal waste management and why they call it "*indoor plumbing.*"

To say I was exhausted would be an understatement. I was ready to ship my two darlings off to Grandma's house. Heck, I would even settle for some peace and quiet at Grandma's myself. All right, maybe a cruise sounds better.

What do your days look like? Do you put in long hours in your profession or job? Are your hours spent as a caregiver? Are you wondering if there is life after diapers? Do you juggle demands of both a family and a career?

When did life get so busy? Do you, like me, get tired just thinking about what lies ahead in your day? Do you measure things by how many minutes they require to accomplish rather than by their importance? Does exhaustion hamper your ability to be the kind of person you want to be?

Both physical demands and emotional stresses can leave us feeling tired, weary, and ready to give up. Financial burdens may leave us feeling weighed down, housework may tax our strength and patience, careers may demand immense energy, and communicating with spouses, children, and others may drain our emotions past the point of empty. Have you felt any or all of these feelings? I have. Some days, life can seem too much to keep up with.

Exhaustion is a subtle blinder. It creeps over us as we try to tend to daily responsibilities and to care for people who depend on us. Usually we don't even see the danger coming until we are ready to break. We can sometimes push ourselves so long and so hard that we feel we have no more left to give.

Not meaning to, we can block the light of the Spirit simply because we are too busy, too weary, and too tired to feel it.

Is running ourselves ragged what is expected of us to please Heavenly Father? Light from the scriptures offers the answer. King Benjamin taught, "It is not requisite that a man should run faster than he has strength" (Mosiah 4:27).

Perhaps you, like me, have thought, "I can't do this anymore!" or "There's no way I can get everything done that I have to get done!" or "I can't keep up this pace!" Well, the good news is that we don't have to get everything done, and we don't have to maintain a breakneck pace. We don't need to do it all, nor should we try to do so.

I've never liked the phrase, "I can't." I've always tried to prove to others that I could do anything I wanted to do—even though I had a visual impairment. If someone told me I couldn't do this or that because I couldn't see well, I would work to prove them wrong.

But I have come to see through the Spirit that it is all right and sometimes very necessary to say, "I can't." It is healthy to have and maintain limits. It doesn't mean we are weak or afraid if we say to ourselves or others, "I can't," or, "I'm sorry; I can't do that activity right now," or, "I can't get everything on my list done today, so what can I postpone or even eliminate?" or, "I'll need to say no this time."

Now, I know there are some things that cannot be eliminated—things and people who must be attended to. I'm not saying that we will have lives of calm serenity because we have set limits. As I tell my boys, "I'm blind, not stupid."

What I am saying is that we will have more exposure to the light of the Spirit if we "see that all these things are done in wisdom and order" (Mosiah 4:27).

President Thomas S. Monson teaches: "We become so caught up in the busyness of our lives. Were we to step back, however, and take a good look at what we're doing, we may find that we have immersed ourselves in the 'thick of thin things.' In other words, too often we spend most of our time taking care of the things which do not really matter much at all in the grand scheme of things, neglecting those more important causes" ("What Have I Done for Someone Today?" 85).

Because I don't have the kind of physical strength that I used to, I have to evaluate constantly the amount of energy I can put forth each day. That helps me decide what really needs to be accomplished and what can wait for another time. With the help of the Spirit, I can "step back" and make sure that I'm not spending my time on "thin things."

This can be the same for all of us, even if we enjoy full health. The "order" and necessity of our activities and those of our family members can be decided as we counsel with the Lord, our spouses, and even our children. This is not an easy feat, but we can expect help from our Father as we seek His light and direction.

I love that Heavenly Father does not expect us to do all things and do them absolutely perfectly. You and I can drop that expectation of ourselves. It is the word *diligent* we should focus on: "And again, it is expedient that [she] should be diligent, that thereby [she] might win the prize; therefore, all things must be done in order" (Mosiah 4:27).

This scripture helps me remember that my goal is to return to my Father in Heaven. Each step, each day of my journey should move me progressively closer to Him. He doesn't expect or even want me to "run faster" than I am able. In fact, there may be days when I can't run at all. I may just be able to walk, crawl, or scoot, but my job is to be "diligent" or faithful as I move forward—no matter how small my progression.

We don't have to be running ourselves ragged to feel like good members of the Church or to be accepted of the Father. Instead, we can follow the inspiration and promptings from the Lord and feel His reassurance and approval. We will not remain in the darkness of physical or emotional exhaustion if we continually seek heaven's light to help us recognize our limits, prioritize daily activities, and even slow down when possible.

Chapter 15

FACE THE SON BY NOT GIVING UP ON GOD

Light-Blocker: Resentment

Throughout my years in Primary and Young Women classes, I learned about and even sang of the "ideal family." Each righteous Latter-day Saint young woman would someday marry a righteous Latter-day Saint returned missionary in the temple. They would be completely faithful to one another, and together they would raise a righteous, happy family. That is the plan, right?

What do we do, then, when less-than-ideal circumstances and challenges arise, and our lives don't turn out how we planned or hoped?

Have you ever found yourself sitting in church feeling like a second-class citizen because you didn't think you fit the "Mormon mold"? Do you find yourself not wanting to attend meetings because you feel uncomfortable, left out, unwanted, or alienated due to your marital or family status? Do you find resentment creeping into your heart and clouding your vision?

At one time or another, we may all struggle with such feelings.

But if you and I give in to these thoughts, then we are allowing darkness to displace the light. Satan, our enemy, wants us right in this position. Why? Because if we hold onto these feelings, let them fester inside of us, and avoid those places where we will receive spiritual light and truth, then our spiritual vision becomes dim. The adversary wants us to misunderstand truth—truth taught by our prophets and apostles. He encourages us to become angry, bitter, and resentful.

How do we reconcile our current family life situation with what we learn at church, and not give into Satan's tactics? I believe the first step is to seek gospel truth and learn God's pattern through the help of the Spirit. Then, with that light, we can understand why there is an "ideal" spoken of so often.

Elder Jeffrey R. Holland explains this with his "parable of the homemade shirt." In his youth, when money was tight, Elder Holland's mother, a talented seamstress, often made clothing for her children to wear to school. She would look at clothes in a catalog or store window and remark, "I think I can make that."

"While she could study the commercial product and come close," Elder Holland said, "what she really wanted was a pattern. A pattern helped her anticipate angles and corners and seams and stitches that were otherwise hard to recognize. Furthermore, if she went back for a second or a third shirt, she was always working from a perfect original pattern, not repeating or multiplying the imperfections of a replica."

Elder Holland continued, "We are bound to be in trouble if a shirt is made from a shirt that was made from a shirt. A mistake or two in the first product—inevitable without a pattern—gets repeated and exaggerated, intensified, more awkward, the more repetitions we make, until finally this thing I'm to wear to school just doesn't fit" ("General Patterns and Specific Lives," 3).

We need a pattern. We must have a pattern to which we can shape our lives. Of course, our marital and family situations vary, and we may have to make adaptations where necessary, but we can agree on Heavenly Father's pattern.

All too often, I wonder if we look at our lives and believe we've failed if we haven't already duplicated the pattern. But with clear vision, which comes through facing the Son, we will see that is not the case. Again, Satan wants us to feel resentful and hopeless. If he can get us to feel this way, then we will grow angry at God and give up by taking our eyes off the pattern.

Heavenly Father, on the other hand, desires our happiness and wants us to keep striving toward the ideal. The Lord has said, "I will give unto you a pattern in all things, that ye may not be deceived" (D&C 52:14).

How can we please our Heavenly Father or even try to become like Him if we have no idea of the divine expectations He has for us concerning marriage and family life? The ideal, or pattern, acts as a guide and a protection. Instead of avoiding or resenting the lessons that teach of God's ideal, we can rejoice that He has revealed His pattern to us.

Each of us has been hurt in our lives. We may feel like giving up on Heavenly Father because it seems He's forgotten us or His promises to us. We may want to disbelieve our patriarchal blessings because we can't possibly see how God will work things out. We may want to stop going to church, praying, or reading our scriptures because those things don't seem to make any difference. Whatever has caused the hurt, the solution is not to turn away from Heavenly Father. The solution is ultimately found in Jesus Christ, His Atonement, His doctrine, "the word which healeth the wounded soul" (Jacob 2:8).

In my youth and early twenties, I honestly wondered if

I would ever get married. Not only did I have eye problems, but my face was deformed because of my childhood radiation treatments. Every guy I got close to seemed to run away because of either my looks or my sight impairment. The chance that any man would ever love the whole me seemed tantamount to pigs flying.

Although I was wary, I could have become bitter toward men in general, and I could have resented the constant teachings at church regarding celestial marriage and forever families. Sure, I had my many moments of frustration, but I knew that Father's plan was correct—even if I had to wait until the next life for my time to be married.

This knowledge didn't take away all of the pain and sadness, but it helped me trust Father in Heaven. I knew that He could not lie, and that He would keep his promises. It was because of this that I kept striving toward the ideal.

The plan of happiness is all about progression. We have not failed if we do not already live in the "ideal family." We fail only when we give up, stop striving and pressing forward (see 2 Nephi 31:20), and do not keep the covenants we have already made.

Christ will help us each step of the way as we continue journeying forward. We have every reason to act. We have every reason to hope. Our current situations may seem impossibly distant from our ideal goal, but Jesus Christ, through His Atonement, can bridge the gap if we remain fixed in our commitment to Him and to His gospel.

I know we will be directed by the Holy Ghost in the ways we need to adapt the general pattern to our individual and specific needs.

We can have complete confidence that our circumstances are known to the Lord. Consequently, we will rid ourselves of blinding resentment toward His ideal and toward Church leaders who teach that ideal. We can and will attend our meetings, not to compare our lives with those of others but to renew our baptismal covenants, to gain spiritual strength and resolve, and to learn of Father's divine pattern, which will enable us to dwell with Him. We will not give up. We will be faithful and strive toward the ideal established by our Father.

Chapter 16

FACE THE SON BY JUMPING IN

Light-Blocker: Going through the Motions

For some time, one of my sons had been stuck in the lovely preteen anti-personal-hygiene phase, and it was a constant battle to convince him that a shower was truly quite necessary. One particular day, he finally conceded and went into the bathroom and closed the door. I heard the shower water turn on and then the shower curtain slide into place. Now, it would appear that he was getting the job done, but the water didn't sound right. It didn't sound like he was actually *in* the shower.

So I opened the bathroom door, and there was my son—outside the shower—fully dressed.

"What?" he asked defensively.

"It might help if you got *in* the shower. You might actually get clean."

He had been caught, and he knew it. The suspicions that I had harbored for several days had been proven correct. My darling son had faked showering for who knows how long. Any time I had asked if he had showered, he had said, "Yes. Feel my hair." His hair had always been wet, but he hadn't really done the job. This smart little boy had only been going through the motions to fool his mother, who didn't have the ability to see. Additionally, due to the severing of my olfactory nerve in an invasive surgery, I couldn't smell him either.

On another occasion, after being asked repeatedly to brush his teeth, my son again entered the bathroom. I heard him open the medicine cabinet, turn on the water in the sink, and make swishing noises with his mouth. After a while, he spat in the sink and tapped on its edge. What did he think, that I was stupid? I might not be able to see—I might have to depend nearly solely on my hearing—but come on!

"It'll work better if you use a toothbrush and actually put it in your mouth," I called.

"Oh, man!" was the next sound I heard from the bathroom.

I wondered why he would go through all the trouble to

make it appear that he was doing what was expected when, if he had just performed each action fully, he would have been the one to gain from the results—not to mention all those who could smell him. It was silly.

Might not this relate to us spiritually? Are we ever guilty of just going through the motions? Do we say prayers instead of communing with the Father through prayer? Do we simply go to church, or do we go humbly to renew our covenants by partaking of the sacrament? Is attending the temple something to check off of our to-do list, or do we go to worship and serve? Do we read the scriptures, or do we "feast upon the words of Christ" (2 Nephi 32:3)? Is home or visiting teaching something we do to not feel guilty? Do we show up once a month in order to report satisfactory statistics, or do we truly love and serve those we teach as the Savior would? Do we live an LDS lifestyle, or do we try to live a Christlike life as a Latter-day Saint? Are we only active in the Church, or is the gospel of Jesus Christ fully active inside of us?

Now, of course, having righteous habits in our day-to-day lives is extremely important and will bring light to our spirits, but why settle for *good* spiritual vision when we could have *great*? If we grow comfortable with the status quo, and merely go through the motions with our spiritual habits, we will be like my son with his "showering." We will not be fully in the water—the living water.

One way we can daily receive the living water is to study the scriptures. I have loved the scriptures ever since I can remember, and am so grateful for the blessings I have received by studying them.

I remember calling home as a college student, just to talk to my mom when things were hard. She would listen, and I would cry and explain whatever difficulty I was facing at the time. Inevitably, our discussion would lead to the scriptures. It didn't matter what the problem was, the solution was always found within those holy pages. Through my mother, I was comforted and taught by the Spirit and the words of ancient prophets.

For me, the scriptures have become a haven. Sure, there are days when I do more reading than feasting. But whenever I study with a prayer and an open heart, I learn truth, receive courage and comfort, and feel connected to the Lord. It isn't always even the words themselves that teach me, but it is the Spirit that is able to work inside me because I am taking time for the feast.

It can be the same for each of us. If we make a sincere effort, Father will bless, comfort, and teach us through the scriptures.

Thus far, we have discussed ways to refrain from negative

thoughts, feelings, and habits that might eclipse the light of the Son. However, I now invite you to be even more proactive in seeking that light. Jump in! Immerse yourself even more in the gospel of Jesus Christ. Take full advantage of the warmth, direction, and light available through the Atonement of our Savior. He is ready to enfold you with His love. Believe Him. Trust Him. Follow Him—not just with outward appearance, but with your whole heart.

As you and I offer the Lord our all, we will feel His love more deeply, and we will see more clearly spiritually. For, He promises, "I am the light of the world: he that followeth me shall not walk in darkness, but shall have the light of life" (John 8:12).

Chapter 17

FACE THE SON BY RELYING ON CHRIST'S ATONEMENT

Light-Blocker: Not Feeling Like Enough

Our plane was to leave at seven o'clock in the morning, so my friend Hilary Weeks and I planned on leaving our homes in Lehi at five in order to be at the Salt Lake City airport by six. We were to participate in a Time Out for Women event in Pittsburgh, and I worked hard to ensure that I hadn't forgotten anything. I was all ready and packed when Hilary and her husband, Tim, came to pick me up. Tim dropped us off at the airport, and everything went smoothly until we checked in.

Hilary said casually, "Kris, have you done something different to your eye?" Kind of like someone might say, "Have you lost weight?" or, "Have you changed your hair? Because you look different." I reached up to touch my eye prosthesis. To my horror, I had no eyeball.

Now, the prosthesis I wear on my right side is made from silicone, and it adheres to the skin covering my eye socket. Because of the way my eye had to be removed when I had cancer, I was unable to wear a normal artificial eye. With this ocular prosthesis, the eyeball can be inserted and removed from the silicone and can be transferred to my alternate when necessary. I had grabbed the wrong prosthesis—the one that didn't have the vitally important eyeball inside.

I burst out laughing. What was I going to do? I couldn't travel across the country and speak to thousands of women in Pittsburgh with no eyeball! I mean, there is a limit to using visual aids. Luckily I had remembered my thinking cap, and so I suggested a plan.

Hilary called her husband, Tim, and said, "Uh, honey, Kris forgot her eyeball. Can you go get it?" I was laughing loudly in the background, and Hilary started busting up as well.

I phoned my husband, James, woke him up, and—between spurts of laughter—asked him to grab my eye and meet Tim halfway. They would make the handoff and Tim would race it back to us at the airport—hopefully before our plane left.

Next, Hilary and I made our way to the security area,

and Hilary tried to explain to the security worker that she would need to come back through after taking me to the gate. "Um, my friend is blind and has forgotten her eye at home. I have to meet my husband out front to get it. Will I be able to get back through quickly, or will I have to go back through the whole security check?"

I tried to do my part by looking blind. I didn't need to do much. After all, I had a fake-looking plastic thing with a gaping socket glued to my face. I'm sure the security guard thought he had now seen everything. He wasn't moved, and he explained very solemnly what Hilary would need to do. We were then off to the gate.

I wasn't going to suffer through another embarrassing explanation, so I sat with some of the other Time Out for Women speakers who had already arrived while Hilary spoke with the gate agent. She went through the whole "My friend is blind and left her eyeball at home" story. Hilary asked them to please hold the plane for her, and then she began her part of the last leg of the eyeball relay.

Soon, our flight was called, and my friend Mary Ellen and I tried to carry our luggage and Hilary's to the gate, where we ran into a slight problem.

"Excuse me," the airline worker said. "You may not take that many bags on board."

Then, from across the way, the agent Hilary had spoken

with called out, "It's all right. She's the one without the eye-ball."

Once seated on the plane, I tried to pull myself together. I tried not to worry, but I imagined James and Tim passing each other going opposite ways on the freeway, throwing the prosthesis across the median like a football. (Little did I know that James hadn't bothered to put the eye in a bag or anything. He just plopped it into Tim's hand and said, "It's sturdy!" Poor Tim.)

I prayed that, wherever they met, the handoff would be made in time for Hilary to catch the plane, and eventually she arrived. Thank heavens the eyeball relay was successful and over!

I had tried my best to make sure I was completely ready for this trip, yet problems still occurred. Isn't that the way life goes? We work our hardest, but our efforts aren't always enough. On this particular occasion, I could laugh about my predicament; however, there have been times when it has saddened and discouraged me that my best wasn't good enough.

I really believe that this is an important part of mortal life's design. When we come to the realization that we can't do everything perfectly on our own—and that we aren't meant to—we can choose to remain frustrated, or we can humble ourselves before our Father. Our humility brings us light and power through the Atonement of Jesus Christ. We may not have enough strength, but He does. We may not be able to handle all things, but He can and did. We may not be enough, but He is. Christ makes our efforts, our abilities, and even ourselves, enough.

Speaking to the women of the Church, Elder Jeffrey R. Holland promised, "Yours is the work of salvation, and therefore you will be magnified, compensated, made more than you are and better than you have ever been as you try to make honest effort, however feeble you may sometimes feel that to be" ("'Because She Is a Mother,'" 37).

I know this is true. I have felt this compensating power often in my life.

I have felt it often lately as I stand and speak in front of audiences. Father has blessed me with more physical energy and strength than I have, and I am able to fulfill my speaking assignments even when I'm sick. I have also begged Heavenly Father to emotionally make me strong enough to share very personal things in order to help other people who may be listening to my message. He never lets me down. Each time, "the Lord stood with me, and strengthened me" (2 Timothy 4:17). He always makes me more and helps me do more than I can alone. That compensation has been light and hope to me.

Our ability to see by the Spirit is improved as we allow

our Savior to make us more than we now are. As we face the Son and put our lives in order with His commandments, He will make us more—more capable, more holy, and more whole. He will make us enough.

CONCLUSION

I s seeing a need or a want?" This was the discussion question in a class I attended at the School for the Blind. I thought my teacher had lost it. Of course, it was a need. Was she crazy?

In my mind, I understood the concept that my teacher, who was also blind, was presenting, but my heart was harder to convince. Breathing and eating were needs, but she taught us that seeing was only a wonderful want. How would I persuade myself to believe and feel this?

I was devastated with the loss of my eyesight. Everything was altered, and life as I knew it had crumbled down around me. I wanted things to return to normal, and the only thing that would enable this was to see. I needed to see! Without my vision, I wasn't sure I could go on.

Years have now passed, and I have adapted to my life in the dark. Although I wish I could see, I now know that seeing is not a need. It is a want. Who thought I would ever feel this way? I never thought I could live being blind, but I have for many years. I now know that I can live a happy, productive life—even without sight.

The ability to see spiritually, however, is definitely a need for me. Without the light from the Son, I would feel hopeless. My mind and heart would never have been able to find the peace that comes through the warmth of the Spirit. I would have never been able to move forward, nor found joy again, without the strength and comfort of my Savior.

With the Son, I have received deep and much-needed healing. Christ has healed my sorrowing heart and troubled mind. He has broadened my perspective and given me hope through His resurrection.

I too will be resurrected, and I will see again through perfected eyes. But, in the meantime, I have the opportunity to improve my spiritual vision. This cannot be done on my own. I will see more clearly only when I face the Son and receive His light. It will take His touch to work the miracles I will yet need in my life.

When Christ healed the beggar in the New Testament,

He did more than heal the man's actual eyes that day. He also healed his brain. This was necessary so that it could process the new images, colors, and dimensions flooding in. Because his mind had known only darkness, it too needed the light from the Master's touch. The Savior, with His infinite wisdom and power, saw the whole need and provided the complete miracle.

He offers the same to each of us. The Savior knows our whole need for healing. In fact, He waits for each of us to turn to Him so that miracles can be worked for our benefit—so He can make us whole.

Christ now stands ready, with perfect love, to offer His divine light. This light is available to you and to me, if we turn and face Him—if we face the Son. If we desire to live with Him again, turning to Christ so we can have clear spiritual vision is not only a wonderful want, it's a necessity.

In partnership with Christ, you and I can feel His light daily and gain strength, comfort, and courage. As we work to eliminate those things that stand as light-blockers to our spiritual vision, He will help us to remember and to fulfill our divine role as Father's children, so we can overcome the "natural man" emotions, thoughts, and behaviors we experience (see Mosiah 3:19). Through His power and our efforts, we can choose a higher way and improve our ability to see.

The obstacle of loneliness will be diminished as we

face the Son and follow the promptings of the Spirit. As we trust God's promises and seek truth from the Source, we will overcome fear and self-criticism. Sadness will be burned away with light from gratitude, and we can look forward with hope in good things to come. Our complaints will become productive when we turn them into prayers, and discouragement will fade as we listen to the encouraging words of living prophets.

As we turn to Christ, we will learn to live vertically and avoid the trap of comparison. Our vision will be clearer as we leave judgment to the Lord and look on the hearts of those around us. The gift of discernment will help us fight irritation, and choosing not to become offended will bring additional light as we let go of anger. The dangerous light-blocker of pride will be reduced as we come to accept the help and service of others, and facing the Son will teach us wisdom in our lives. This wisdom will help us to prioritize our days and to minimize exhaustion, leaving us more able to feel the promptings of the Holy Ghost.

Even when we are tempted to become and remain resentful, we can choose the light that comes with not giving up on God. On those days when it seems that we are spiritually just going through the motions, we can make an increased effort to jump into the gospel of Jesus Christ. We then will be in a better position to receive the blessings of the Atonement. Through the power and grace of Jesus Christ, He can make us more than we are. He can and will make us enough.

Through the voice of the Spirit, we will be able to identify other light-blockers, and by facing the Son, we will receive light to know how to overcome them. We will become more like the Savior each time we choose to turn to Him and obey His will. In the process, our spiritual vision will be sharpened and, eventually, perfected.

Jesus Christ truly is "the light of the world" (John 9:5), but He can become more than this. I invite you to allow Christ to be your *personal* light. Turn to Him. Face the Son. Allow Him to flood your life with His marvelous light.

SOURCES

Bednar, David A. "And Nothing Shall Offend Them." *Ensign*, November 2006, 89–92.

———. "Quick to Observe." *Ensign*, December 2006, 31–36.

Children's Songbook. Salt Lake City: The Church of Jesus Christ of Latter-day Saints, 1989

Hinckley, Gordon B. "The Light within You." *Ensign*, May 1995, 99.

Holland, Jeffrey R. "'Because She Is a Mother.'" *Ensign*, May 1997, 35–37.

———. "The Best Is Yet to Be." *Ensign*, January 2010, 22–27.

———. "General Patterns and Specific Lives." *Worldwide Leadership Training Meeting: Building Up a Righteous Posterity*, February 9, 2008.

SOURCES

Holland, Jeffrey R., and Patricia T. Holland. *On Earth as It Is in Heaven*. Salt Lake City: Deseret Book, 1989.

Kimball, Spencer W. "President Kimball Speaks Out on Service to Others." *New Era*, March 1981, 46–49.

Monson, Thomas S. "What Have I Done for Someone Today?" *Ensign*, November 2009, 84–87.

Parkin, Bonnie D. "Choosing Charity: That Good Part." *Ensign*, November 2003, 104–6.

Smoot, Mary Ellen. "Rejoice, Daughters of Zion." *Ensign*, November 1999, 92–94.

Uchtdorf, Dieter F. "Happiness, Your Heritage." *Ensign*, November 2008, 117–20.

INDEX

INDEX

INDEX